ME AND THE SKY

Captain Beverley Bass, Pioneering Pilot

By **BEVERLEY BASS**
with Cynthia Williams

Pictures by
JOANIE STONE

Alfred A. Knopf
New York

This is a story that begins with a stubborn little girl with one thing on her mind—flying! She would climb up on her family's washing machine and jump off, her arms outstretched like wings. She fell and bruised her knees, but she climbed right back up and tried again.

Her name is Beverley Bass.

When Beverley was a baby in a stroller, she squealed and reached with both hands for airplanes flying overhead.

When Beverley got a little older, she talked her aunt Ginger into taking her out to the airport at night to watch the airplanes take off and land.

When she was a little older still, Beverley asked her daddy if she could take flying lessons when she turned sixteen. He shook his head. He was sure that flying was only the passing fancy of a little girl with a big imagination.

But Beverley would not give up on her dream. Remember the washing machine? She looked up into the sky and knew she had to go there. It was such an unusual aspiration for a young girl that she didn't talk about it much with her friends. But her determination never wavered.

When she was nineteen, Beverley decided she could wait no longer. She drove herself to the airport and signed up for flying lessons.

Beverley had been flying in airplanes since she was little. Just walking into the small airport terminal in her hometown of Fort Myers, Florida, got her heart beating fast. And when the engines revved and the propellers whirled and the plane began rolling down the runway, faster and faster, Beverley's heart swelled up so much she thought it would burst.

Her heart was pounding the day she climbed aboard the small trainer plane for her first flying lesson. She had no idea her instructor was going to let her hold the controls. She wrapped her hands around the yoke. At last, she was where she had dreamed of being all her life—in the pilot's seat of an airplane!

Beverley had always been fascinated by how tiny everything looked from an airplane, and it was even more striking when she was the one doing the flying. She gazed down at the tops of trees and at cars so small they looked like toys. She saw houses with tiny swimming pools and tinier people. They flew over the beach. Look! White seagulls floating way down below the plane. Beverley's smile grew so wide that tears came to her eyes. She felt as if she were floating.

When she got home that evening, Beverley said to her parents, "I am going to fly for the rest of my life."

She was a natural—fearless, confident, and eager to learn. It wasn't long before Beverley was allowed to fly all by herself, with no instructor aboard the airplane. When she flew over her house, her mother would run outside and wave. Her parents were proud of their daring daughter.

Beverley wanted to do more than just fly for fun. She wanted to be an airline pilot, the kind who wears a uniform and flies big airplanes filled with people. What an idea! Everybody knew airline pilots were men, not *girls*. People felt safe in planes flown by men. Who would feel safe with only a girl in the cockpit? This is the way people thought when Beverley was growing up, not so very long ago.

But Beverley was stubborn. Remember the washing machine? She kept taking lessons until she got the licenses she needed to fly cargo. She took jobs that men didn't want. She took jobs that men left behind when they got better ones. And in this way, she, too, moved on to better jobs, like flying private planes for businessmen.

Again and again, Beverley proved that she could do anything men could do. She showed people that it doesn't take big muscles to fly airplanes; it takes brains and determination, and she had plenty of both.

And at last, her chance came. American Airlines was hiring pilots. In those days, all pilots started out as flight engineers or copilots. A flight engineer sits behind the copilot in the cockpit and ensures that all the systems that make the aircraft fly are working properly. It is a great responsibility. Very few women in the United States had held that position. Would American Airlines trust a twenty-four-year-old woman with such a job?

They did.

Two years later, Beverley moved up a seat, right next to the captain of the airplane. She had been promoted to copilot and was now one of only a handful of women in the United States who were first officers aboard a major passenger carrier!

A few years after that, Beverley's lifelong dream came true. She moved up once more—into the captain's seat. At the age of only thirty-four, Beverley Bass made history as the first woman ever to captain an American Airlines commercial airliner.

When they gave Beverley her silver captain's wings, her heart filled with pride, and her eyes with tears of gratitude.

On one of her first flights as captain, Beverley flew into her hometown airport. The man who had let Beverley hold the controls on her first flying lesson was there to meet her, along with her parents, news reporters, her third-grade teacher, her lifelong best friend, Laurie, and a hundred other people.

At her departure, as the jetliner 727 began to roll down the runway, the crowd grew quiet, watching through the big glass window of the terminal. Their heads turned together as the jet rushed past them. Captain Bass eased the throttles forward, the nose of the plane lifted, and the roar of a hundred voices rose with it.

The little girl who used to jump off her mother's washing machine grew up to make history. She was the first female captain of an American Airlines B727 and then of an American Airlines B767. She was the first female to captain an all-female flight crew for American Airlines and was also their first female check airman—air*woman!*—teaching other pilots to fly their big aircraft.

Oh, and the little girl who was told that girls can't fly big airplanes? She was the first female to command a Boeing 777, the largest twinjet in the world for an airline.

"Never let anyone tell you that you can't," Beverley says. "'Can't' is the worst word in the English language. Believe in yourself and know that you can do anything you set your mind to." Beverley's life teaches us that dreams can come true, but not by wishing; dreams come true through hard work and determination. Her message is simple: "No dream is too big. Dream big and soar high!"

BEVERLEY BASS, TRAILBLAZER

Beverley in her American Airlines uniform in 1986.

The story of Beverley Bass is the story of a young woman who blazed a trail in the sky for the many women who have followed in commercial aviation.

In 1910, a French actress named Elise Raymonde de Laroche became the first woman to earn a pilot's license, but sixty years later, when nineteen-year-old Beverley Bass took her first flying lesson, women were still only allowed to fly private planes, never commercial airliners. All over the world, records were being broken for women in aviation, but as late as 1970, getting past the gender barrier in commercial aviation in the United States remained a seemingly impossible feat. It wasn't until 1973 that the airlines hired their first female pilot. Her name was Emily Howell Warner, and in 1976 she became the first woman captain of a U.S. commercial airliner.

In that same year, when Beverley won her seat as a flight engineer for American Airlines, she was their third female pilot, but two years later, she became the first female to fly an American Airlines B727 as a first officer, or copilot.

In 1986, Beverley was the first female captain for American Airlines. And in 1999, Beverley Bass became the first female captain of a Boeing 777, the world's biggest twinjet, in an airline operation.

She was eminently well qualified, therefore, for the in-air emergency she would face only two years later.

September 11, 2001

On the morning of September 11, 2001, Captain Bass was flying an American Airlines jumbo jet home from Paris, France, to Dallas, Texas. She was at 39,000 feet, approaching forty degrees west longitude over the North Atlantic, when she heard, over her pilot's special radio frequency, that a plane had hit one of the World Trade Center towers in New York City. Twenty minutes later, she heard that a second aircraft had hit the other tower. Captain Bass ordered a lockdown of the cockpit.

New York airspace was closed. By now, the world knew that these two planes and two others had been hijacked by terrorists, and the government was putting fighter aircraft into the air to stop any more attacks. As Captain Bass neared her destination, she saw an unprecedented aviation phenomenon. International carriers around her were making 180-degree turns and heading back to Europe.

It wasn't just New York; all of U.S. airspace was closed. Any airplane crossing into U.S. airspace now would be shot down.

At fifty degrees west longitude, as she exited Atlantic international waters, Captain Bass made voice contact with Gander Air Traffic Control, which directs traffic at a small airport in Newfoundland, Canada. The response was immediate. Circumventing established protocol, the controller issued an order.

"American four nine, proceed direct to Gander and land immediately."

They were the thirty-sixth plane to land in Gander that day. This small community of some 9,400 people was frantically preparing to receive, in the next few hours, almost 7,000 passengers from thirty-eight international airliners.

Beverley's son, Taylor, and daughter, Paige, shortly after September 11, 2001. While Beverley was in Gander, her family anxiously awaited her return at home in Texas.

Come from Away

Gander Air Traffic Control, on a moment's notice, managed the unprecedented task of guiding thirty-eight jumbo jets, with thousands of passengers, to their airport in a three-hour time frame.

Simultaneously, the town instantly mobilized buses and taxis, customs officials, police, and Red Cross workers. Business owners and homeowners opened their arms and homes, restaurants, and shops without reserve or hesitation to the stranded passengers. Bus drivers, who had been embroiled in a strike, immediately suspended it. Local residents dashed into their kitchens and started cooking, running platters of food, as well as blankets, pillows, and extra clothing, to the airport and to emergency shelters. Everyone in Gander, the locals and the "plane people" alike, formed a lasting bond that week.

Beverley and her husband, Tom, at the play's opening night in Los Angeles.

Fourteen years later, the story of the kindness and generosity the people of Gander showed to Beverley, her crew, and the passengers, and those of the other thirty-seven commercial jetliners that landed there that day, became a musical, titled *Come from Away*. Written by David Hein and Irene Sankoff, the play premiered in California's La Jolla

Playhouse in June 2015 and toured several major cities, breaking box-office records around the country. In March 2017, *Come from Away* opened on Broadway.

The play is a sensation. It has won many awards, including five Outer Critics Circle Awards. Every night, it plays to full houses and receives weeping standing ovations.

Central to this beloved production is the character of Beverley Bass, played by Jenn Colella, who received a Tony nomination and won one of the show's five Outer Critics Circle Awards for her memorable portrayal.

Beverley (right) with Jenn Colella, who portrays her in the Broadway musical.

Beverley's Legacy

In 1977, not long after Beverley first became an airline pilot, she thought it would be fun if, once a year, all the women airline pilots in the country got together. So she and a friend, Stephanie Wallach, a pilot for Braniff Airways, founded the International Society of Women Airline Pilots. The first ISA convention was held in Las Vegas in 1978. All forty or so women flight engineers, copilots, and captains were invited, and twenty-one showed up. Those twenty-one women are the charter members of ISA today. What a sight they must have been in their uniforms for people who didn't know there were any women airline pilots in the world at all!

Today, ISA has 600 members. It is a nonprofit organization offering career support and mentoring to both active and aspiring women pilots; its charitable and educational mission has awarded over $1.3 million in advanced flight scholarships to women.

Pioneering women aviators like Captain Bass, whose will to succeed led them to break down the barriers to women in aviation, have given full-throttle forward to the careers of women who dream today of becoming commercial and combat pilots, astronauts, and aerospace engineers.

And that is how a determined little girl, jumping off a washing machine in an attempt to fly across the kitchen, winged her way into history.

Members of ISA, with Beverley front and center, attend a performance of *Come from Away*.

To Molly Sankoff Hein and "her people" —B.B.

For Yvette, may you always reach for the stars —J.S.

THIS IS A BORZOI BOOK PUBLISHED BY ALFRED A. KNOPF

Text copyright © 2019 by Beverley Bass
Jacket art and interior illustrations copyright © 2019 by Joanie Stone
All rights reserved. Published in the United States by Alfred A. Knopf, an imprint of Random House Children's Books, a division of Penguin Random House LLC, New York.
Knopf, Borzoi Books, and the colophon are registered trademarks of Penguin Random House LLC.
Visit us on the Web! rhcbooks.com
Educators and librarians, for a variety of teaching tools, visit us at RHTeachersLibrarians.com
Library of Congress Cataloging-in-Publication Data is available upon request.
ISBN 978-0-525-64549-8 (trade) — ISBN 978-0-525-64550-4 (lib. bdg.) —
ISBN 978-0-525-64551-1 (ebook)
The text of this book is set in 16-point Latienne Roman.
The illustrations were created digitally.

MANUFACTURED IN CHINA
September 2019
10 9 8 7 6 5 4 3 2 1
First Edition

Random House Children's Books supports the
First Amendment and celebrates the right to read.